THE MAGICAL ART OF
SURREAL ROMANTICISM

THE MAGICAL ART
OF
SURREAL
ROMANTICISM

Oliver St. John

TANTRIKA BOOKS

ANNO V–2 ΘΕΛΗΜΑ

The images of Tarot Atu I, *The Magus of Power*, and *Traces of King Arthur* by Ithell Colquhoun, are reproduced in this book by courtesy of the Artist's Estate.

With thanks to Soror V. A. A. for kindly allowing us to take a high resolution scan of *Sabbath*, from a sketchbook of Austin Osman Spare, for inclusion in this book.

The original Salvador Dali Tarot painting collages are owned by Distribucions d'Art Surrealista. Other original artworks are kept in various private collections and galleries around the world.

TANTRIKA BOOKS

www.tantrika.co.uk

You endow art with mystery by not knowing what you are doing.

People do not choose Surrealism. Surrealism chooses them.

Jan Švankmajer

Contents

Illustrations

I

A Babe in the Egg of Blue

Throughout the long dark history of humanity there have been magi. While some are known for their works, be it art or literature, there must be countless men and women that have either failed to develop their innate gift or have succeeded in mastering it while keeping silence to the end. Of those that fail to develop the gift (or curse)—whether by refusing it, fleeing from it in horror or becoming insane, there is little to be said. Of those that master it, whether partially or fully, some are known and others will never be known since they did not utter a word.

The word of a magus is irrevocable, as we shall see, though it is said that failure to utter a word is equally irrevocable since it must beget an abortive child. The momentum of the immense forces that first push the soul onward and then draw the soul inexorably *inward* towards annihilation of ego identity is sufficient to split the atom or, in psychic terms, to fragment the soul until its very name is forgotten and it endures dispersion and ultimate oblivion.

The magical child, however, of which it is the object of the art of magical alchemy or of the Great Work to produce, is not the result of any cause. The ancient chestnut of determinism has become a poisoned apple in the hands of modern philosophers and rationalists. The magical child of consciousness—otherwise termed the True Will—grows as a seed in the silence of the womb of the cosmic Matrix. The fruit and the flower, nonetheless, has preexisted the seed. For this reason, the magi have oft been reported as stricken with awe at the sight of a portentous star where no star previously was seen, or plunged into rapture at the sight of a wild orchid blooming in a desert where a single drop of rain would amount to a miracle.

In many respects this book is a vindication of the work of the English scholar and mystic, Thomas De Quincey, famed for his book, *Confessions of an English Opium Eater*. Many persons mistakenly believe the *Confessions* to be a book about opium, or opium addiction. It is quite common for critics to mix their appreciation for the work with offhand rebukes. It is as though the writer, in spite of all he wrote in his own defence and his tireless efforts to explain what his work is really about, must automatically be an unreliable witness since he is accused (and therefore must surely be guilty?) of drug addiction. Horror of horrors! Better not let him in here, then, not in our house. "A remarkable talent", they say, "What an intriguing and curious saga", and "But oh! how shameful his vice, he might have achieved so much more." Thomas De Quincey's knowledge of the Greek and Latin classics was his holy Qabalah; his use of etymology was *mantic*, the means of subtle conveyance. Language was his brush, words the pigment with which to stain the canvas of memory, experience and love.

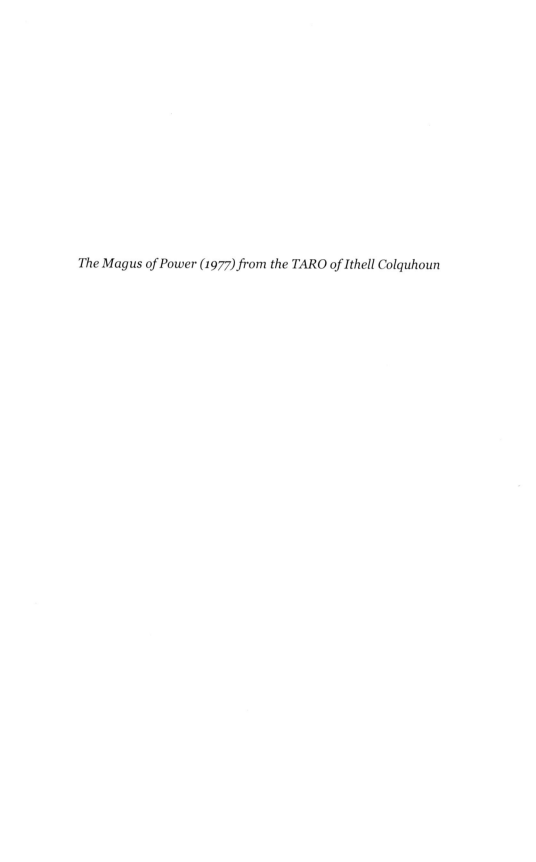

The Magus of Power (1977) from the TARO of Ithell Colquhoun

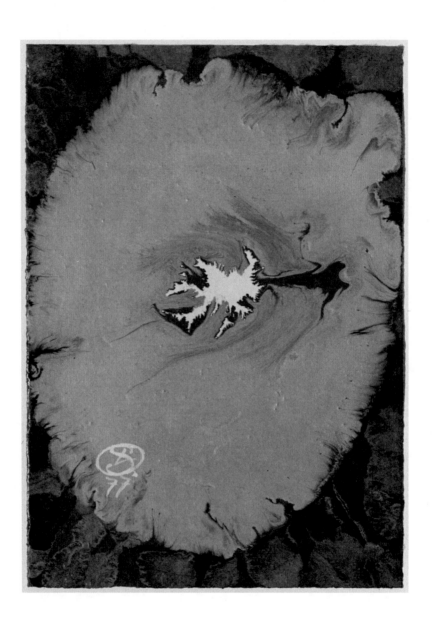

II

Surrealism and the Occult

Automatism in the arts is frequently confused with mere techniques. True automatism is an inexorable condition of mind and soul that to all intents and purposes is exercised outside and beyond the will of the person, whether they are destined to become a master, a magus, or merely another victim swallowed up by an incomprehensible universe. For ordinary purposes, we may define artistic automatism thus:

"The avoidance of conscious intention in producing works of art so that subjectivity forms the primary basis of the work."

Automatism was not an invention of the Surrealists, or of Sigmund Freud, but has always existed in magick and alchemy. Among the finest examples are the sigils or magical *signatures* of the Qabalistic Intelligences and Spirits of the planets as given by Cornelius Agrippa in *Three Books of Occult Philosophy* (1531) and centuries later copied into *The Magus*, by Francis Barrett (1801). These beautiful designs, along with other more abstruse signatures that can be found in medieval grimoires, were written on virgin parchment by the hand of the spirit, not that of the scribe. We also have the evidence of the Enochian language received through the invocations and skrying of Elizabethan mage John Dee and his assistant seer, Edward Kelley.

Automatic writing as a spiritual practice was reported by Hyppolyte Taine in the preface to the third edition of his *De l'intelligence* (1878). Portuguese poet and writer Fernando Pessoa (1888–1935) reported having etheric visions, and that he could see magnetic auras.

Pessoa also said that he experienced automatic writing, and that he felt "owned by something else", sometimes feeling a sensation in the right arm which he claimed was lifted into the air without his will. Unfortunately the material nature of many such accounts—especially those of the Spiritualist movement—have lent ammunition to the firing squads of those sceptics and rational science dogmatists infected with missionary zeal. The latter have been quick to confuse automatism in the clinical sense with the work of poets, philosophers and mystics. Notably, the word "automatism" is also used in psychiatry, but there it is used with an exclusively criminal frame of reference, that is to say, performing actions that are not willed, as a defence plea or justification, that the perpetrator was not responsible for their actions. It is the magical, mystical and artistic use of the word that we are concerned with here.

Occult artist and writer Ithell Colquhoun—a friend of André Breton, Aleister Crowley and later, Kenneth Grant—was a member of the Surrealist School. Ithell Colquhoun defined her use of automatism as *super-automatism*, presumably to distinguish the method from the same term that is used in psychiatry and law. We shall from hereon adopt the term as used by Colquhoun, *super-automatism*, when we are referring to spiritual, magical or artistic method or even natural inclination.

Within the modern Hermetic magical tradition there are some notable examples of *super-automatism*. George Hyde-Lees, the wife of William Butler Yeats, claimed that she could write automatically. W. B. Yeats' *A Vision* originated during the afternoon of 24th October 1917, when he and his wife experimented with automatic writing (four days after their wedding). Earlier in the century, Aleister Crowley claimed that he magically received, through the mediumship of his wife Rose, the Egyptian Book of the Law, Liber AL vel Legis, in Cairo 1904.

Page 1 of Liber XXX: Holograph MS of Liber AL vel Legis (1904)

Had! The manifestation of Nuit

The unveiling of the company of heaven

Every man and every woman is a star

Every number is infinite; there is no difference

Help me, o warrior lord of Thebes, in my
unveiling before the Children of men

Be thou Hadit, my secret centre, my
heart & my tongue.

Behold! it is revealed by Aiwass the
minister of Hoor-paar-kraat

The Khabs is in the Khu, not the Khu in
the Khabs

Worship then the Khabs, and behold my
light shed over you.

The Book of the Law is art of a completely different order than the complex and somewhat unwieldy work of *A Vision*. When the Book of the Law was first received, Crowley added a note to the manuscript saying:

"This is a highly interesting example of genuine automatic writing."

Aleister Crowley later insisted the book was dictated by a praeterhuman intelligence named Aiwass, his Holy Guardian Angel. In fact, there need be no essential contradiction between magical *super-automatism* and contact with a praeterhuman agency. Crowley was very sensitive, however, as to how the book might be viewed by posterity. He did not want what he considered to be his most important work compared with drawing room séances and psychism.

Chapter One, verses 1–8 of the Book of the Law (facing page) reads as follows:

Had! The manifestation of Nuit.

The unveiling of the company of heaven.

Every man and every woman is a star.

Every number is infinite; there is no difference.

Help me, o warrior lord of Thebes, in my unveiling before the Children of men!

Be thou Hadit, my secret centre, my heart & my tongue!

Behold! it is revealed by Aiwass the minister of Hoor-paar-kraat.

The Khabs is in the Khu, not the Khu in the Khabs.

Worship then the Khabs, and behold my light shed over you!

The writer and occultist Dion Fortune (Violet Firth, 1890–1946) produced a work of *super-automatism* entitled *The Cosmic Doctrine*. The work was not published until three years after her death, 1949, but became central to the teaching and practice of the Fraternity of the Inner Light, which Dion Fortune founded. *The Cosmic Doctrine* is a complex cosmology in which the atom is used as a metaphor for the soul. Anyone familiar with the work of Dion Fortune will see it was not a product of ordinary thought, though it is elegantly structured and rational. In the author's own words:

"This volume of teaching was received from the Inner Planes during 1923 and 1924. The one who gave it is a human being evolved to a very high level. The Personality of his last incarnation is known but is not revealed, but it may be said that it was of a world-famous philosopher and teacher. In the terminology which is used in esotericism this individual is one of the 'Greater Masters.' "

It hardly needs mentioning that Dion Fortune, in common with many other occultists of the 20th century, believed in the popular myth of personal reincarnation, and was also undoubtedly influenced by the writings of Helena Petrovna Blavatsky. It is by now a well established fact that Blavatsky invented "Hidden Masters" or "Secret Chiefs" to camouflage her political interests, and those of the (living) Hindu sages that supplied the information from which she worked up her *Secret Doctrine*. None of that, however, need invalidate the work of *The Cosmic Doctrine* as a remarkable testimonial to the "avoidance of conscious intention in producing works of art so that subjectivity forms the primary basis of the work". Such questions as to whether *The Cosmic Doctrine* has any real practical import or use must ultimately be determined by the student; as a literary and occult work of art it does not bear comparison with any other.

Sabbath (1954), Austin Osman Spare (sketchbook)

Artist Austin Osman Spare (1886–1956), who was associated with both Aleister Crowley and occult writer Kenneth Grant, used *super-automatism* in drawing, painting, and in the creation of magical scripts and even textual narratives. As *super-automatism* has been used in magical and Hermetic disciplines since time immemorial it can readily be seen why Surrealist artists shared ideas in common with occultists. Automatism is sometimes compared to free association, a method used by Sigmund Freud to plunder the so-called unconscious mind of his clients. The French poet André Breton, who published the *Surrealist Manifesto* in 1924, became aware of automatism through the work of Freud. Breton here defined Surrealism as follows:

"Psychic automatism in its pure state, by which one proposes to express—verbally, by means of the written word, or in any other manner—the actual functioning of thought. Dictated by thought, in the absence of any control exercised by reason, exempt from any aesthetic or moral concern."

The method used by Breton and others involved writing down as rapidly as possible anything that comes to mind. Thus modern automatism began as a literary method. Artist Max Ernst supplied the 'first' visual automatism by making collages from sections cut out from magazines, catalogues, advertisements or anything else that was available. Other painters enthusiastically took up automatism, from Joan Miro, André Masson and Ithell Colquhoun to Jackson Pollock, noted for his development of abstract expressionism. Although automatism is usually regarded as a separate method from that which Salvador Dali termed *paranoiac critical*, the end or object is really the same. *Paranoiac critical* can be defined as:

"The artist invoking a paranoid state with the intention of deconstruction of the psychological concept of ego-identity."

Paranoia is taken to mean the fear that one is being manipulated or controlled by others. This may of course include the paranoid manipulation of others. Some of the tricks that Dali liked to play were very much inclusive of the 'audience', so the boundaries between who was doing what to whom were blurred, increasing the paranoia for all concerned! The aim of the method, however, is that *subjectivity becomes the primary basis of the work*. It is to defeat the rational mind, prohibitions and censorship that stem from ego.

Ithell Colquhoun

Ithell Colquhoun (1906–1988) described her work as "mantic". Mantic means, "pertaining to divination or prophecy", and is derived from the Greek, *mantikos*, "divination", *mantis*, "prophet". Unlike other artists, Colquhoun deliberately wished to connect Surrealism with magick, both philosophically and in terms of method or technique. In her own writings she drew comparisons between visual art and the medieval art of alchemy.

Colquhoun wanted to achieve a union of natural and spiritual forces as well as a union of the disciplines of art and the occult. She suggested that the four traditional elements of Hermetic magick (as cited by Agrippa, for example) might each have corresponding automatic methods:

△	Fire	Fumage
▽	Water	Écrémage and parsemage
△	Air	Blowing or fanning powdered materials
▽	Earth	Decalcomania

The union of subject and object, the I-Self with all that is 'other', the Not-Self, is the goal of yoga or *union*, and is a prerequisite for magick and mysticism at advanced levels. Notably, Colquhoun created a set of 78 Tarot cards using the method of *super-automatism* to produce entirely abstract images. Her method was to pour enamel paint onto a horizontal support of paper or card, wet paint on wet paint, tilting, stirring and conjuring the layers of colour to react and interact.

The strength or degree of dilution of the paint would be carefully decided beforehand to reflect the key colour scales of the Four Worlds of the Hermetic Tree of Life: Atziluth, Briah, Yetzirah and Assiah. The interaction of the colours would then facilitate spontaneity, lending them depth and brilliancy. Colquhoun might use the wooden end of a paintbrush to manipulate or introduce additional colours or highlight a feature, but always retaining the integrity of the automatic state, which she described as a light trance. Essentially, the forms and images were influenced by forces that were not under Colquhoun's conscious control. The cards were to be used as meditation *yantras*, and the esoteric titles of the cards, for example, *The Magus of Power*, were used as *mantras* to induce vision and higher states of consciousness—it was therefore integral that the card's images should emerge from and clearly reflect the same. She went on to produce paintings of the ten sephiroth or emanations of the Qabalistic Tree.

Ithell Colquhoun was associated with numerous magical Orders. As well as painting and drawing, she wrote several books, including *The Sword of Wisdom*, an exposé of the Golden Dawn tradition of magical occultism. Early in her career, Colquhoun assumed the magical name or motto *Splendidior Vitro*. The motto appears as a monogram on each of the 78 Tarot cards in her Surrealist deck. This translates as "brighter than crystal", or "clearer than crystal".

Ithell Colquhoun's magical name was presumably taken from the Odes of Horace, 3: 13, that begins, *O fons Bandusiae splendidior vitro...*

Oh Bandusian fountain, brighter than crystal,
Worthy of sweet wine, not without bloom,
Tomorrow we'll honour you with a goat,
Whose brow is budding
With horns destined for love and battle.
All in vain: since this child of the playful herd will
Darken your ice-cool waters
With the stain of its crimson blood.
The dread hour of flaming Sirius
Knows no way to touch you; you offer your lovely
Coolness to bullocks, weary of ploughing,
And to wandering flocks.
For you are born of the noble spring—how can I speak
Of the holm oak that's rooted above
The hollow in the rock where your
Clear babbling waters run down?

III

Prophets, Seers and Sages

There is far more to *rhabdomancy* or "water divining" than merely using rods to determine the physical location of a hidden spring. The springs and fountains in question are the waters of space, cosmic consciousness and the mysterious current of life itself. When the natural flow of the life force is sent backwards to its source, union with the infinite is made possible. This has ever been the goal of yoga, and even prayer when that is understood in the true sense, but there are methods and techniques that greatly accelerate progress.

Kenneth Grant (1924–2011) has alluded to *Vajroli Tantra* and the *Varma Marga* or Left-hand Way of the East in his Typhonian Trilogies, and also made use of the expression, *retroversion of the senses.* Occultist and novelist Gustav Meyrink (1868–1932), known for his brilliantly inspired first novel, *The Golem,* referred to the 'backward way' of *Vajroli Tantra* in the dénouement of his *Angel of the West Window,* loosely based on the life of the Elizabethan magus John Dee. As in the case of automatism in the arts, we are entering an area where confusion exists between mere techniques and a very ancient spiritual and magical path of knowledge. To employ the outer methods without knowledge of the inner keys is to throw straws in the wind and hope to build a palace.

Swami Vivekananda

There is a peculiar kind of scepticism, especially virile in England and Europe, which is only comfortable with mystic rapture if it comes from the East—the further away, perhaps, the better. Heaven forbid that a man or woman born in England should confess to mystic rapture! The life and work of any European mystic from the 19th century to the present day is usually put down to either drug addiction or insanity.

Even 19th century Aestheticism was controversial at the time—now it is only taught or discussed as a historical footnote. The word "aesthetic" is derived from the Greek word *aisthetikos*, itself formed from *aistheta*, "perceptible things"—the *Perceptible* that is conveyed by means of the *Intelligible. Aisthesthai* generally means, "to perceive" or " to sense". It is not merely the perception of sense-objects but is the apprehension of the meaning *behind* the appearance of visible nature. To put the reader at ease, I will provide an anecdote from one of the great Indian sages that had a great deal of influence on Western minds, Swami Vivekananda (1863–1902), or Naren as he was known to his friends.[1] At the age of fifteen years, Naren's family had to travel for two weeks across country from Bengal to Raipur in the Central Provinces. Part of the journey was made in bullock carts, where they traversed dense forests full of wild animals. In the words of Swami Vivekananda:

"What I saw and felt as we passed through that forest has always remained printed on my memory. And one day more than all the others. It was the day we skirted the lofty range of the Vindhya hills. The peaks on either side of the road rose very high into the sky. On the slopes, the trees and creepers were wonderfully beautiful; heavy with fruit and flowers. Birds of all colours were flying from grove to grove or swooping to the ground in search of food, and filling the gorge with sweet cries. Seeing all this, I felt an extraordinary peace of mind. The slowly moving chain of bullock carts reached a place where two great rocks had come together in an embrace like lovers over the narrow forest trail. Looking around me attentively at the point where they met, I saw that there was a very deep cleft from the top to the bottom of the rock on one side of the trail and that, inside the cleft, there hung an enormous honeycomb; the result of the bees' labour throughout many years."

---

[1] The birth name of Vivekananda was Narendranath Dutta.

"Filled with wonder, I thought about the kingdom of the bees—how it had begun and how it had ended—and my mind became so deeply absorbed in the thought of the infinite power of God, ruler of the three worlds, that I lost all consciousness of my surroundings for some time. I don't know how long I lay in the bullock cart in that condition. When I regained external consciousness, I found that we had passed that place and were already far away. As I was alone in the cart, no one ever knew this had happened to me."[2]

Thomas De Quincey (1785–1859)

A prophet is not without honour, but in his own country, and among his own kin, and in his own house.

Gospel of Mark, 6: 4

Automatism is no more an invention of Sigmund Freud than the Greek myths are an invention of Carl Jung. The method has been used by writers, poets and mystics since time immemorial. However, Carl Jung privately practiced the art of alchemy, as did Albert Einstein. Both men placed inconceivably deadly weapons in the hands of children. In the case of Jung, the weapon was the analytical sword of reason, applied to the human soul. In the case of Einstein, the weapon was the atom bomb.

Psychoanalysis rests on the assumption—appealing finally to vain hope!—that it can cure the afflictions of human souls through placing them under professional guidance. Thanks to this rationalist universal panacea, millions of persons now actually believe it is possible to be 'happy', 'confident', or 'balanced', and that it is even worth pursuing such banal agendas.

---

[2] *Ramakrishna and his Disciples*, Christopher Isherwood.

Personal psychological happiness or wellbeing flies in the face of the self-evident collective psychosis of the entire race. Psychoanalysis aims to produce an individual that is better adjusted to social and economic systems that depend on war, genocide and wholesale destruction of the environment for their continuance. The belief in psychological happiness is thus predoomed to strengthen self-delusion; the scale of woe is increased while all the while the one precious chance of immortality runs away like sand through an hourglass. To illustrate the rationalist *mantram* we shall provide a quotation from a psychoanalytical study of the Whispering Gallery and the Bore from Thomas De Quincey's 1856 Revision of *Confessions of an English Opium Eater*. The italics are mine, not the author's:

"The text conceptualizes the idea of psychoanalysis as a mobile scene of confrontation with the mesmerizing influence of the unconscious, but also as a psychoanalysis mesmerized by its own functioning. The Whispering Gallery and the Bore symbolize how the telling and thus the naming of psychic *determinism* within autobiography of 1856 reinforces this *determinism* as a textual figure for how interminability has not been overcome. Consequently, this *determinism* turns *merely digressive passages* into symptoms of an addiction to telling that replaces the purpose of confession altogether."[3]

The word "determinism" is here repeated with hypnotic insistence. The analyst, intent on interpreting the work as evidence of psychopathology, sets up his victim by firstly predefining his thought and behaviour according to arbitrary values. He then engages with the assault while manifestly entranced by the very disorder he is accusing his victim of suffering, namely, "an addiction to telling that replaces the purpose of confession altogether".

---

[3] *Romantic Psychoanalysis: the Burden of the Mystery* (pp. 172), by Professor Joel Faflak.

Euclid (1945), Max Ernst

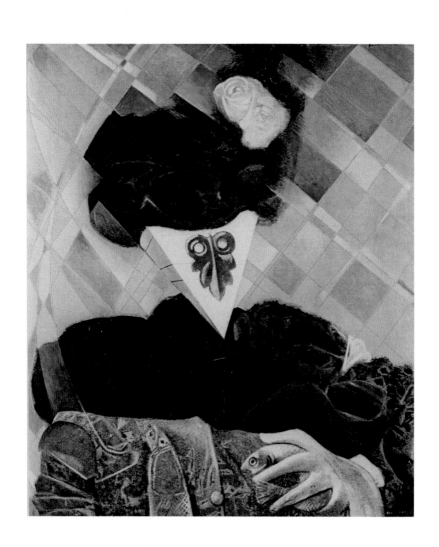

The analytical study conveys the impression that since the subject under discussion is entitled, "Confessions", the writer and visionary Thomas De Quincey must, *ipso facto*, have had a psychoanalytical agenda in writing it. While the baneful flower of psychoanalysis was certainly rooted in the late Romantic period historically, De Quincey wrote the book and the revisions long before the term "psychoanalysis" even existed (1890s). Thomas De Quincey was a very spiritual man by natural inclination—that is, he had no desire or interest in pursuing the phantom of psychological happiness or wellbeing. Determinism is usually seen as a philosophical contradiction of 'free will', and so De Quincey's theme, of an ominous inevitability issuing from an eternal or transcendent realm, is misconstrued by the psychological or analytical thinker as resulting from determinism—a line of thought that is deterministic in itself. Philosophical determinism, an ancient debate concerning whether there is or is not such a thing as 'free will', is itself a confusion between destiny, fate, inevitability and causality. In his own words, De Quincey recollects his experience in the Whispering Gallery of St Paul's Cathedral, London:

"That consideration [of consequences not foreseen] saddened me, and deepened more and more the ominous suggestion— the oracle full of woe—that spoke from those Belshazzar thunderings upon the wall of the Whispering Gallery."

It was not the intention of Thomas De Quincey to place his soul on the couch of the psychoanalyst that assumes the role of ventriloquist, with the patient as dummy. The analyst goes on to insist that the 1856 Revision contains "merely digressive passages". This depends on the ability of the reader to comprehend De Quincey's backward flow of thought, his fast-flowing stream of literary and etymological illustrations. In like fashion, an unsophisticated person might look at a canvas by Max Ernst and see nothing but randomised scrawls and etching.

In the words of Thomas De Quincey (*Confessions*):

"If a man 'whose talk is of oxen', should become an opium-eater, the probability is, that (if he is not too dull to dream at all)—he will dream about oxen."

Generations of critics have no doubt seen De Quincey's horror and outrage at the wanton destruction of ancient woodlands in England and Wales for the purpose of building roads—even in the middle of the 19th century—as "merely digressive". The Whispering Gallery and the Bore passages from De Quincey's 1856 Revision nonetheless provide a mystic key to the narrative of De Quincey's famous book. The key is in the Latin warning that he cites in the Whispering Gallery account:

Nescit vox missa reverti, "A word once uttered is irrevocable".

It is helpful to quote at length from De Quincey's 1856 Revision. Here is the passage that gives full account of the Whispering Gallery episode:

"As an oracle of fear I remembered that great Roman warning, *Nescit vox missa reverti* (that a word once uttered is irrevocable), a freezing arrest upon the motions of hope too sanguine that haunted me in many shapes. Long before that fifteenth year of mine, I had noticed, as a work lying at the heart of life and fretting its security, the fact that innumerable acts of choice change countenance and are variously appraised at varying stages of life—shifts with the shifting hours. Already, at fifteen, I had become deeply ashamed of judgments which I had once pronounced, of idle hopes that I had once encouraged, false admirations or contempts with which I had once sympathised. And, as to acts which I surveyed with any doubts at all, I never felt sure that after some succession of years I might not feel withering doubts about them, both as to principle and as to inevitable results."

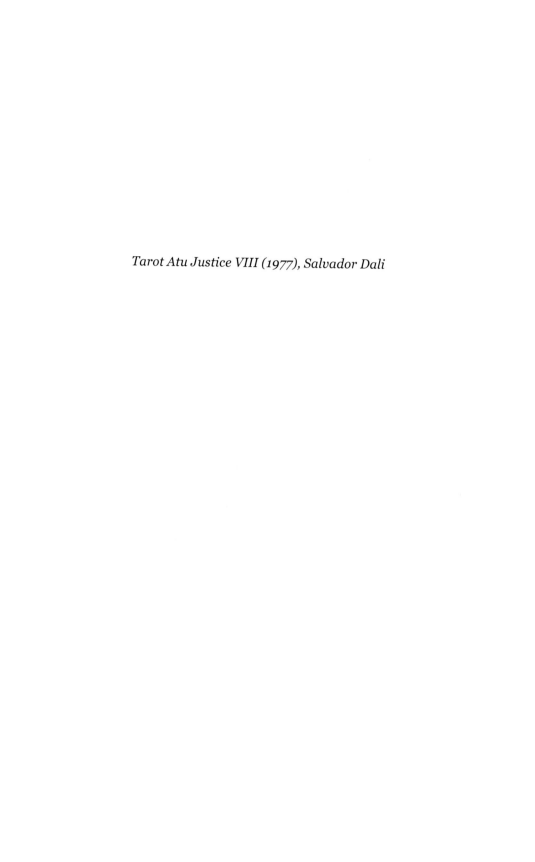

Tarot Atu Justice VIII (1977), Salvador Dali

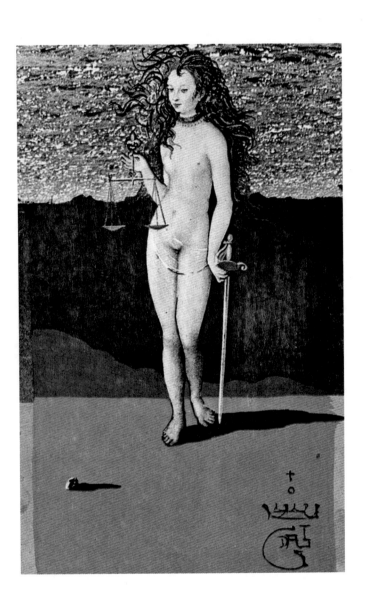

"This sentiment of nervous recoil from any word or deed that could not be recalled had been suddenly re-awakened on that London morning by the impressive experience of the Whispering Gallery. At the further end of the gallery had stood my friend, breathing in the softest of whispers a solemn but not acceptable truth. At the further end, after running along the walls of the gallery, that solemn truth reached me as a deafening menace in tempestuous uproars. And now in these last lingering moments, when I dreamed ominously with open eyes in my Manchester study, once again that London menace broke angrily upon me as out of a thick cloud with redoubled strength; a voice, too late for warning, seemed audibly to say, 'Once leave this house, and a Rubicon is placed between thee and all possibility of return. Thou wilt not say that what thou doest is altogether approved in thy secret heart. Even now thy conscience speaks against it in sullen whispers; but at the other end of thy long life-gallery that same conscience will speak to thee in volleying thunders.' "

Note that De Quincey, who was was well acquainted with the Bible, uses the words, "as out of a thick cloud". The expression, "thick cloud", occurs six times in the biblical Old Testment, usually in the context of divine utterance. The Aramaic word is ONN (*onan*), which is etymologically related to OVNN, "To do magick or perform a conjuration; a magician". The "cloud" is also a mystic metaphor for the *Shekinah* or female Holy Spirit—the visible, natural or supernatural manifestation of the divine presence.

The defining quality of *super-automatism* is that once the dream or vision is fully encountered by the visionary, it is never forgotten—it cannot be sent back. This, by the way, refutes the whole basis of psychoanalysis, which is that by a process of professionally guided recollection and confession, the soul can be cured of its afflictions.

If Thomas De Quincey had by chance been born an Indian prince, or lived his life in the foothills of Tibet, he would no doubt have acquired a reputation as a great sage. As it was, he was born in England in the Romantic era and could not do otherwise than reflect the *miasma* or cumulative psychosis of his time and place. In spite of De Quincey's seemingly untiring efforts to explain his *Confessions*, the book is still mistakenly supposed to be a book about drugs, since some of it deals with the intensification of thoughts, dreams and visions through the use of opium.

De Quincey's insistence that he experienced visions long before he discovered opium falls on deaf ears among editors and readers alike. De Quincey spent a good deal of time explaining and justifying his work to critics that failed to grasp what he energetically strove to convey—that the realm of the immortal is *within the reach* of human beings, and is not some abstraction to be accepted or rejected according to the whim of the intellect. Or, it might be said, of any critic.

The architecture of the Whispering Gallery is such that the merest whisper uttered at one end is magnified and heard with thunderous echoes at the other end of the gallery. De Quincey's experience in the gallery, of his friend "breathing in the softest of whispers a solemn but not acceptable truth", is central to his thesis: that all words, deeds, and even dreams, are not only never forgotten but may also recur with fulminating force.

While a common dream, a vain or futile life, might be forgotten in time, it is the *intensity of experience* that determines whether a soul lives, is immortal, or dies the death of being *forgotten*. Thomas De Quincey used the word "impressive" to describe his experience, not in the sense that his account of it might strike awe into the heart of the reader, but in the root meaning of the word, from the Latin *imprimere*, from whence "imprint": to design or make an imprint; a seal or stamp. A further meaning of the word is to fix an idea in the mind, so it is remembered.

Traces of King Arthur (1957), Ithell Colquhoun
(illustration for Living Stones—Cornwall)

IV

Phallus of Cosmic Recollection

According to the ancient Egyptian mystery tradition, to achieve immortality the soul must be remembered by Thoth, or Sesheta, his female predecessor. Thoth and Sesheta are the personification of time itself; they are the keepers of the Book of Life or Akashic Record. The 'name' of any soul—the unique signature or vibration of that soul—must be written in the Book of Life if it is to endure. To be forgotten is to die the death of oblivion. It is thus an error to assume that recollections dismal or disturbing, or that bring fear in their wake—compounded all the more by the quality of their magnetism—are a symptom of malaise, or even of personal failure. It is not the phantoms of fear or imagining that endure, but the consciousness that is not only able to observe them but that also holds the power to *evoke them at will*. As it was put in the ceremonies of the late Romantic era Hermetic Order of the Golden Dawn:

"By names and images are all powers awakened and reawakened."

The power of the word is the same power otherwise called "magick". The word and the image, imagining or divine *Imagination* as termed by William Blake, are one and the same. The phallus is the symbol of the extension of the will, a word that in its Greek origin (φαλλος) also means "image" or "image-making". Such a word, image or Logos should not be thought of as exclusively the province of the male member, or of the reasoning faculty, though there has been much confusion owing to the nature of the symbolism. The divine Creatrix is the primary type of the Logos, a feminine personification of the generative principle and the eternal Tree of Life from which all gods and men are sprung.

Both male and female experience tumescence while in the nocturnal dreaming state—a fact that was well known to the ancients who depicted all gods of the underworld (i.e., the subconscious realms) as holding the phallic or generative power. This key has clearly been lost, as evidenced by the attempts of scientists to explain ancient artefacts. Any unearthed images depicting ancient gods or goddesses are invariably described by these learned men and women as "fertility symbols".

The usual abode of dreaming is the night. Hence Thomas De Quincey concludes the section on the Whispering Gallery with the following—even though he has been insistent that he was able to *dream while fully awake*:

"A sudden step upon the stairs broke up my dream, and recalled me to myself. Dangerous hours were now drawing near [nightfall], and I prepared for a hasty farewell."

We now move on from the fiery fountain of Swami Vivekananda's vision of the honeycomb, and the airy fountain of sonic vibration as described in Thomas De Quincey's Whispering Gallery, to the watery fountain of *rhabdomancy*, "divining by rod". Here, De Quincey describes the *backward flowing* stream of consciousness that embodies the aim of *Vajroli Tantra*. De Quincey introduces *rhabdomancy* as a metaphor when giving an account of "forms of darkness shrouded within the recesses of blind human hearts". For most persons, the "solemn evening service of the English Church—read by Mr. Lawson" might affect nothing more than a cure for insomnia, but to the sensitivities of De Quincey, long before he became acquainted with opium:

The Obscure Gods (1947), Max Ernst

"Already in itself, without the solemnity of prayers, the decaying light of the dying day suggests a mood of pensive and sympathetic sadness. And, if the changes in the light are less impressively made known so early as five o'clock in the *depth of summer tide*, not the less we are sensible of being as near to the hours of repose, and to the *secret dangers of night*, as if the season were midwinter. Even thus far there was something that oftentimes had profoundly impressed me in this evening liturgy, and its special prayer against the perils of darkness. But greatly was that effect deepened by the symbolic treatment which this liturgy gives to this darkness and to these perils. Naturally, when contemplating that treatment, I had been led vividly to feel the memorable *rhabdomancy* or magical power of evocation which Christianity has put forth here and in parallel cases."[4]

De Quincey goes on to explain that the ordinary physical diviner merely wishes to find the earthly location of a hidden water well, or of minerals, "or hidden deposits of jewels and gold", by magnetic sympathy between the magick rood or wand and the occult object of divination. He then speaks of a higher or more sublime form of *rhabdomancy*, by which magnetism may call up from the darkness, "sentiments the most august, previously inconceivable, formless, and without life", so exalting their character as to "lodge them eternally in human hearts". Furthermore, the "mysterious path of winds and tempests, blowing whither they list, and from what fountains no man knows, are cited from darkness and neglect, to give and to receive reciprocally an impassioned glorification, where the lower mystery enshrines and illustrates the higher."

---

[4] The italics are mine, not those of the author—except in the case of *rhabdomancy*.

Before introducing the anecdote we have previously explored, the Whispering Gallery, De Quincey tells how the prayer against the darkness *automatically* evoked for him the very thing it was meant to quell!

"Night and Darkness, that belong to aboriginal Chaos, were made representative of the perils that continually menace poor afflicted human nature. With deepest sympathy I accompanied the prayer against the perils of darkness—perils that I seemed to see, in the ambush of midnight solitude, brooding around the beds of sleeping nations; perils from *even worse forms of darkness* shrouded within the recesses of blind human hearts; perils from temptations weaving unknown snares for our footing; *perils from the limitations of our own misleading knowledge.*"

The Bore is a backwards flowing tidal surge that Thomas De Quincey encountered while standing on an artificial mound called the Cop by the river Dee, outside Chester. Owing to certain peculiar conditions, a tidal wave surges *backwards* along the river Dee—backwards to its source. This filled De Quincey with indescribable dread and horror. In the Whispering Gallery, the backwards surge was the power of Logos, the whispered utterance from one end of the gallery and received, according to De Quincey, as "Balshazzar thunderings" at the other end.

De Quincey likens the end of the gallery to the *end of life.* The experience of the Bore is clearly related to the fountain of life itself, in this case experienced as chaotic and hostile. While De Quincey's account of the Bore is undoubtedly one we can classify under the classical or alchemical element of water, it is nonetheless the sonic vibration that plays a central role in his experience. He therefore places emphasis on this by the repeated use of descriptive nouns such as "clamour", "outcry", and "sea-like roars":

"From this unseen reach it was that the angry clamour, so passionate and so mysterious, arose: and I, for *my* part, having never heard such a fierce battling outcry, nor even heard of such a cry, either in books or on the stage, in prose or verse, could not so much as whisper a guess to myself upon its probable cause. Only this I felt, that blind, unorganised nature it must be—and nothing in human or in brutal wrath—that could utter itself by such an anarchy of sea-like roars. What was it? Where was it? Whence was it? Earthquake was it? Convulsion of the steadfast earth? Or was it the breaking loose from ancient chains of some deep morass like that of Solway? More probable it seemed that the *ano potamon* of Euripedes (the flowing backwards of rivers to their fountains) now, at last, after ages of expectation, had been suddenly realised. Not long I needed to speculate; for within half a minute, perhaps, from the first arrest of our attention, the proximate cause of this mystery declared itself to our eyes, although the remote cause (the hidden cause of that visible cause) was still as dark as before. Round that right-angled turn which I have mentioned as wheeling into the next succeeding reach of the river, suddenly as with the trampling of cavalry—but all dressing accurately—and the water at the outer angle sweeping so much faster than that at the inner angle, as to keep the front of advance rigorously in line, violently careered round into our own placid watery vista a huge charging block of waters, filling the whole channel of the river, and coming down upon us at the rate of forty miles an hour. ... In fact, this watery breastwork, a perpendicular wall of water carrying itself as true as if controlled by a mason's plumb-line, rode forward at such a pace, that obviously the fleetest horse or dromedary would have no chance of escape. Many a decent railway even, among railways since born its rivals, would not have had above the third of a chance."

"Naturally, I had too short a time for observing much or accurately; and universally I am a poor hand at observing; else I should say, that this riding block of crystal waters did not gallop, but went on at a long trot; yes, long trot—that most frightful of paces in a tiger, in a buffalo, or in a rebellion of waters. Even a ghost, I feel convinced, would appal me more if coming up at a long diabolical trot, than at a canter or a gallop. ... The praeternatural column of waters, running in the very opposite direction to the natural current of the river, came up with us, ran by with the ferocious uproar of a hurricane, sent up the sides of the Cop a salute of waters, as if hypocritically pretending to kiss our feet, but secretly understood by all parties as a vain treachery for pulling us down into the flying deluge; whilst all along both banks the mighty refluent wash was heard as it rode along, leaving memorials, by sight and sound, of its victorious power."

De Quincey transforms his experience of standing on the mound called the Cop into an eternal symbol. This may be compared with two irrationally constructed Greek words that appear in Aleister Crowley's Egyptian Book of the Law, Liber AL vel Legis, III: 72:

"I am the Lord of the Double Wand of Power; the wand of the Force of *Coph Nia*—but my left hand is empty, for I have crushed an Universe; and nought remains."

The Egyptian Book of the Law was, by Crowley's own confession on the front page of the holograph manuscript, received by something akin to *super-automatism*. *Coph Nia* (Σοφ Νια) may be considered as the Qabalistic Ain Soph reversed; the Ain Soph, "limitless and without form", is a key part of Qabalistic cosmology, and constitutes a veil preceding the formulation of light or projected consciousness.

When the flow of consciousness is reversed it turns away from matter, the appearance of thoughts and things, and returns to the numinous source or absolute. The crushing or destruction of a universe is well known to those familiar with the terminology of Tantrik cults. Knowledge reaches its apotheosis in the meditative trance of *Shivadarshana*, as it is termed in the Tantras.

De Quincey's reference to the *ano potamon* of Euripides reveals his meditation is upon the waters of life in the spiritual sense (*potamon hudatos zoes*), or in the sense of eternity. It is the flowing backwards of *consciousness* that is here indicated, a Tantrik or Left-hand path method not to be confused with regression or recollection in the psychological sense. Thomas De Quincey's insights need to be understood in context. He has previously described his experience at the Whispering Gallery, where the merest whisper uttered from one end of the gallery is heard as a thunderous roar of echoes at the other end—that is to say, at the other end *of life*. Gustav Meyrink, in his last novel *Angel of the West Window*, employed the river Dee, outside Chester in England, as a metaphor for a magus, John Dee, as one that travels through (and transcends) time and space. Meyrink, like De Quincey, was not concerned with the popular myth of reincarnation but was exploring the imaginative possibilities of *eternal recurrence*.

De Quincey employed a type of *super-automatism*, comparable to Salvador Dali's *paranoiac critical*; in so doing, De Quincey may have endured, and attempted to describe in his writing, the equivalent ordeal in a Rosicrucian Hermetic Order called the Curse of a Magus. Any attempt to describe the indicible is doomed to failure, hence the "curse", for as cleverly suggested by Aleister Crowley in his *The Book of Lies*, there is a certain obligation to speak truth even while knowing full well that it will be fatally misconstrued or otherwise perceived as *alogia* or simple incoherence.

Others will also see the utterer of the truth, the irrevocable word, as a liar, madman or fool. The magus must utter an irrevocable word yet must reverse consciousness to sail a vessel against the flow of time and return to the source of the fountain of all life. To meditate upon Wisdom herself (Σοφια) is to behold divinity face to face, the magical power of Chokmah—it is also to court with madness. According to Thomas De Quincey (1856 Revision to *Confessions*):

"If in this world there is one misery having no relief, it is the pressure on the heart from the *Incommunicable*. And if another Sphinx should arise to propose another enigma to man—saying, What burden is that which only is insupportable by human fortitude? I should answer at once—It is the burden of the *Incommunicable*."

The passage has a remarkable affinity with another verse from Aleister Crowley's Egyptian Book of the Law, Liber AL vel Legis, III: 34:

"But your holy place shall be untouched throughout the centuries: though with fire and sword it be burnt down & shattered, yet an invisible house there standeth, and shall stand until the fall of the Great Equinox; when Hrumachis shall arise and the double-wanded one assume my throne and place."

Hrumachis is a Graeco-Egyptian name for the Sphinx or polymorphous God that assumes different shapes and forms as according to the evolution of man's consciousness over aeons of time. The "fall of the Great Equinox", by the reckoning of the ancient Egyptians, refers to the present time, the precessional Age of Aquarius.

V

Qabalah of the Unutterable[5]

The Latin warning cited by Thomas De Quincey, *Nescit vox missa reverti*, "a word once uttered is irrevocable", may be abbreviated as a Qabalistic *notariqon*: N. V. M. R. The notariqon yields the number 296 by Hebrew letter values. As a noun, NVMR is the reverse of RMVN, "a pomegranate"— and so the two words are numerically and Qabalistically identical. Rimmon (a corruption of *Ramanu*) is also "The Thunderer", an Assyrian god otherwise known as Ba'al, the son of Ishtar or Inanna. Ishtar descends into the underworld, casting off her seven veils as she passes through them, in order to rescue her son. Ishtar is the original type of the saviour that was in much later times regarded exclusively as the role of a man-god and sacrificial victim.

Rimmon, or Ba'el, was much loathed by the biblical scribes. In the Old Testament, 2 Kings 5: 18, there is a threat made against those who might "bow down in the house of Rimmon"—that is, to pay homage to pagan gods. The biblical text is usually cited as a warning against compromising one's convictions or beliefs. Likewise, the eating of apples or the seeds of the pomegranate, at one time the symbols of life, health, strength and knowledge, eventually became seen as a metaphor for sin and evil—the sin of being disobedient to scriptural laws and prohibitions that were sanctified and made statute by emerging nation states as long ago as the year 500 BCE.

---

[5] The Qabalistic words and numbers underpinning this essay were culled from *The Flaming Sword Sepher Sephiroth* (Ordo Astri), scheduled for publication in 2016 e.v.

The number 296 is also that of KVRO, "curved in upon itself". The Hebrew word is identical to the epithet of the Greek Persephone, the *Kore*. *Kore* means "Maiden", and is etymologically related to *kear*, "heart", and *Ker*, the name of a goddess of fate and death (since good and evil are known in the heart). The principle of *inward turning*, the centripetal motion, is that of the Qabalistic realm of Knowledge or Da'ath. The centripetal force draws the soul inward. Da'ath is also known as the Abyss, for the soul that fears annihilation of the ego and (therefore) personal identity is kept out of the Garden of Eden, the biblical paradise that is guarded by a Flaming Sword that turns "every way" according to the book of Genesis. The turning inward in meditation—or *super-automatism*—is a prerequisite to direct knowledge or Gnosis. For the same reason, magical and Tantrik practices of turning back or turning within have been regarded as sinister and evil for at least two and a half millennia—for direct knowledge always contradicts the dogma of scripture and scientism.

The number 296 is that of TzVR (*Zar*), "a rock or stone". The word also has the meaning of concentration or compacting, and was the name of an ancient Phoenician city. Both meditation and *super-automatism* require inward turning and concentration of the mind—as well as *kear* and *kore*, heart and soul. *Zar* has many variants in our *Sepher Sephiroth*, but like *Kore* and *Rimmon*, it has taken on evil connotations. The word therefore has the further meaning, "stranger or foreigner", which is the primary attribute of Set, the magical Initiator that has been demonised and reviled since scriptural law and science became the only acceptable means of communing with the absolute. The rock or stone of *Zar* is an ancient metaphor for the very foundation and basis of life itself. It is the same stone referred to in alchemical texts such as the *Sophic Hydrolith or Water Stone of the Wise*, in association with the quest for immortality or the elixir of life.

There is a Qabalistic method known to the ancient Egyptians that is given in the Egyptian Book of the Law, Liber AL vel Legis, I: 25, "divide, add, multiply, understand". By this method, NVMR achieves the value of 729:

NVMR-RMVN	=	(296 x 2) 592
592 + 2 (the Dyad)	=	594
594 ÷ 2 (the Dyad)	=	297
297 by *temurah*	=	**729**

The number 729 is that of QRO ShTN, "The Head of Satan" as according to our *Sepher Sephiroth*. The "head" is the beginning as well as the end of life. Such a beginning and end is depicted in the imagery of the Christian crucifixion where Jesus dies on a cross on a hill called Golgotha, "mount of the skull". The head here signifies the sending of consciousness *backwards to its source*—for consciousness is the stream issuing from the fountain of life itself.

Another "head", this time that of Baphomet (BAVOMIThR) according to a spelling worked out by Aleister Crowley, has the value of 729. The Baphomet is an eponymous name for the Outer Head of a magical Order. As *The Devil XV* of Tarot, the symbol is a veil for the Astral Light and a monstrous form of the Sphinx of Nature.

In Gustav Meyrink's *Angel of the West Window*, the Baphomet is a metaphor for the Holy Guardian Angel, not even partially revealed to the Initiate until torturous ordeals have been passed through.

The number 729 is that of the Greek *skaphe* (σκαφη), "ship or vessel", which symbolises a magical or resurrection body for the transportation of consciousness, attributed to the third Qabalistic sphere of Binah. Binah, "Understanding", is beyond the abysmal threshold of human ego consciousness.

Binah may also be considered, in Thelemic terms, as the manifestation of Nuit, the magical *Khu* body surrounding the *Khabs* star. The "star" is the innermost portal of consciousness that is attributed to Chokmah, the natural abode of the magi.

The Greek *eurgesia* (ευεργεσια), 729, is the "perfected work", signifying that the accomplishment or consummation of the Great Work of magick or alchemy is the end (or purpose) of life—for the end is with the beginning, the return to the fount of all.

Finally, 729 is the number of *stugnos* (στυγνος), "abominated". The Curse of a Magus, as according to the writings of Aleister Crowley, is that he must speak the truth—and therefore will be reviled and mocked by others as a liar, a fool or madman.

Note that the reverse Qabalah of NVMR-RMVN (*above*) spells out *Nescit vox missa reverti* as though in a looking glass: "a word once uttered is irrevocable". A magus must utter an irrevocable word; one must reverse *consciousness* to sail a vessel against the flow of time and return to the source of the fountain of all life.

Other Books by Oliver St. John

The Ending of the Words—Magical Philosophy of Aleister Crowley

Hermetic Qabalah—A Foundation in the Art of Magick

Ritual Magick—The Rites and Ceremonies of Hermetic Light

Stella Tenebrae Volume One Number 1

Stella Tenebrae Volume One Number 2

Hermetic Qabalah Initiation Workbook

The Mystic Tarot and the Trees of Eternity

Magical Theurgy—Rituals of the Tarot

Hermetic Astrology

Dedication of a Sanctuary or Temple

The Law of Thelema—Quantum Yoga

In Preparation (2016)

The Flaming Sword Sepher Sephiroth

Ordo Astri (the Order of the Star)

Contact details and information on O∴ A∴ courses and membership availability:

www.ordoastri.org

Made in the USA
Las Vegas, NV
19 July 2022

51845997R00036